MW01034933

UNEDITED VERSION

UNEDITED VERSION

STARTING A BUSINESS
ALLOWING THE HOLY SPIRIT
TO BE YOUR CEO

Sharon Wilson Jawo

WESTBOW
PRESS®
A DIVISION OF THOMAS NELSON
& ZONDERVAN

Copyright © 2016 Sharon Wilson Jawo.

All rights reserved. No part of this book may be used or reproduced by any means, graphic, electronic, or mechanical, including photocopying, recording, taping or by any information storage retrieval system without the written permission of the author except in the case of brief quotations embodied in critical articles and reviews.

All Scripture quotations, unless otherwise indicated, are taken from the King James Version.

This book is a work of non-fiction. Unless otherwise noted, the author and the publisher make no explicit guarantees as to the accuracy of the information contained in this book and in some cases, names of people and places have been altered to protect their privacy.

WestBow Press books may be ordered through booksellers or by contacting:

WestBow Press
A Division of Thomas Nelson & Zondervan
1663 Liberty Drive
Bloomington, IN 47403
www.westbowpress.com
1 (866) 928-1240

Because of the dynamic nature of the Internet, any web addresses or links contained in this book may have changed since publication and may no longer be valid. The views expressed in this work are solely those of the author and do not necessarily reflect the views of the publisher, and the publisher hereby disclaims any responsibility for them.

Any people depicted in stock imagery provided by Thinkstock are models, and such images are being used for illustrative purposes only. Certain stock imagery © Thinkstock.

ISBN: 978-1-5127-6425-3 (sc)
ISBN: 978-1-5127-6424-6 (e)

Library of Congress Control Number: 2016919139

Print information available on the last page.

WestBow Press rev. date: 12/1/2016

Contents

Acknowledgements

Apostle Don Kraft, my Spiritual Father

Apostle Maurice Wright, Spiritual Father

Nona Rogers, my mom

Sankaray Jawo, My loving husband

These four people have had a major impact on my life and are always there to encourage and support me.

Introduction

"What is man, that thou art mindful of him? And the son of man, that thou visitest him? For thou hast made him a little lower than the angels, and hast crown him with glory and honor. Thou madest him to have dominion over the works of thy hands; thou hast put all things under his feet; all sheep and oxen, yea and the beasts of the field; the fowl of the air, and the fish of the sea, and whatsoever passeth through the paths of the seas." Psalms 8:4-8

We have been created with everything we need to live a prosperous life. As God formed us, he placed destiny, authority, and dominion within our human body. We have the capability to operate out of prosperity and to command the earth to line up with our declarations. The glory and honor of the Almighty God is placed in us. The power we possess is strong enough to obliterate every negative and demonic force that comes anywhere close to us. When we allow ourselves to come into the knowledge of God's word, we now hold the key that unlocks the hidden mysteries of Jesus Christ that lies within. The creator of the universe saw fit for me to be on this earth, alive and well, for such a time as this. Oh how wrong of me to not make the best of it. It seems foolish to have a weapon during a battle and to never use the weapon. Others coming against me and maximizing the weapons they have, yet I allow them to defeat me when my weapon is so much more powerful, does not sit well with me. Allowing the enemy to come against you daily and make you feel defeated in every area of your life is equivalent to not using your weapon during a battle. God has given you what you need in order to prosper. We have to look within, find out what is there and learn to use what we have.

Psalms 8:6 have informed me that everything my hand touches, I have dominion of. Everything on the earth is under me. Why does it appear that everything on the earth is above me? Why am I able to see with my eyes the prosperity of others and I'm not able to partake in it? The person across the street seems to be no different than me, why does she have a successful business and people working for her and I do not have either? I'm smart, I'm good; I believe in Jesus, why can I not seem to make ends meet? Everything I put my hands to seem to fail, what am I doing wrong?

You have ideas but you just can't seem to bring them to life. You desire greatness but have no idea on how to achieve it. These are thoughts, millions of people have daily. Today we will declare and decree, nothing shall frustrate the plan of God for our lives. God does not want to see you suffer. Suffering a defeated life is not God's punishment for you.

As you read this book, allow the Holy Spirit to give you revelation of His word. Ask the Holy Spirit to allow you to be sensitive to hear the voice of the Lord, so you may complete this journey of life being and doing what thus says the Lord.

Chapter 1

Entrepreneurship is in Your Genes

"Behold that which I have seen: it is good and comely for one to eat and to drink, and to enjoy the good of all his labor that he taketh under the sun all the days of his life, which God giveth him: for it is his portion. Every man also to whom God hath given riches and wealth, and hath given him power to eat thereof, and to take his portion, and to rejoice in his labor; this is the gift of God. Eccl.5:18-19

Entrepreneurship is the capacity and willingness to develop, organize, and manage a business venture along with any of its risks in order to make a profit. Everything we need to prosper is within each and every one of us. The desire to create or build a business has been given to us by our Creator. Many times these desires are fleeting thoughts because of the lack of knowledge we have concerning our faith. Having our own business is no easy task. The finances, time, and the courage it takes to possess a successful business appears to be inaccessible when we are thinking this through with our natural mind. We have to have the mind of Christ to believe we are more than able to have such great success. Prosperity is not just for everyone else, it's also for me and you.

As we attempt to move forward, in many cases we find ourselves going backwards. Stumbling blocks are there to distract, frustrate, and cause doubt to creep in us. We have to continue to believe that nothing shall frustrate the plan of God for our lives. Standing on this belief daily can help us to know moving forward and pressing through the stumbling blocks are the only options. We have been freely given the gift to be prosperous and enjoy whatever it is we are doing to have a residual income. Today is the time to receive the gift and live accordingly.

Have you ever wondered how different your life will be if you brought your dream to reality? It is so easy to envy the prosperity in others and wish that prosperity was ours. It is possible that we are the very one holding back our desires from coming into fruition. We need to move on our vision and see the manifestation of it come to past. Visualizing a business is much easier than taking the necessary steps to bringing it to fruition. The process of bringing our dreams to life can seem much too complicated to work on. It is challenging, frustrating, and patience is definitely required. However, the end result is rewarding. In order to have those rewarding results, we have to be in a position to be led by God. Wanting God to be the CEO of our business we have to have an ongoing relationship with Him.

My prayer is, *"God show me myself so I can see where to change and lead me in the way of everlasting."* It's imperative to pray such a prayer because many times it's hard to pinpoint the issues in our own lives. But, because we serve a merciful and faithful God, He is ready to lead us into deliverance. I'm now in a position where I can see God showing me how to rid myself of me and see less of me and more of Him in me. Now that I'm looking like the image of God, my Creator, I must think like Him. In order to think like Him, I have to have His word in my heart, mind, and soul. The only way to have this is to have a renewed mind.

Just as God instructed Joshua, He has also instructed us to meditate on His word day and night. Joshua 1:8 tells us the ways to prosperity and a successful life is to not let His book depart from us. Meditating on God's word day and night is a definite way to have a renewed mind. Solomon, David's son was a great man filled with prosperity and wisdom. David instructed him in I kings 2:3, to keep the statues, commandments, judgment, and testimonies that are written in the law of Moses in order to become prosper in everything he does. Because of Solomon's obedience, his mind was renewed. He was a man of faith and he desired what God purposed for him to have. God appeared to Solomon in II Chronicles 1:7 and told Solomon to ask for whatever he wanted God to do for him. God knew he could ask Solomon a question like that because He knew His word was in Solomon's heart. He knew Solomon desired things of the Spirit not of the flesh. If God appeared to us right now and said He will give us whatever we request. What will we request? Will we have a selfish request or will we be like Solomon and ask for what God have purposed for us to have anyway? The only way to know if our hearts are parallel to God's purpose is to read, research, and study His word. Reading the history of Solomon, allows us to know only a certain degree of wealth and wisdom he retained. II Chronicles 1:12 reads, *wisdom and knowledge is granted unto* thee; and *I will give thee riches, and wealth, and honor, such as none of the kings have had that have been before thee, neither shall there any after thee have the like.* We have to study and research the parabolic meanings in His word, the Holy Bible, and that gives us the secret to great prosperity.

To have the living God on the inside of us is more than a confession. If there is power in Jesus, we now have power in us. If there is healing, deliverance, prosperity, courage, creativity, love, and life in Jesus, we possess the same. Today we will start to operate out of Jesus and no longer out of the flesh. We will begin to think from a spiritual perspective and not from human reasoning. We will walk by faith and not by sight. It appears we can't do this but, God said we can. He said all things are possible through Jesus Christ. *"Holy Spirit, I need You to be a daily minute-by-minute part of my existence. Here I am, walk with me, and let me walk in thanksgiving as I receive what the Father has for me today. I want to be sensitive to hear You and maximize every opportunity that comes my way today."* I prayed this prayer when I didn't understand What I was praying, and today this is my reality.

Now we have searched within and communed with our Lord so we are ready to start our business and bring life to those great ideas. There are many books in our library that tells us step by step to starting our business. In today's society we can sit in the comfort of our own home and use technology to research anything we want to know concerning starting a business. Therefore, we no longer have to wait on someone else to answer our many questions we have to get started. We can simply go online and search for all the answers.

The lack of finances is the number one reason people say have stopped them from going forth with their business idea. Money is very important and we have to have it in order to live and be comfortable based on our needs and desires. It may appear to be hard to obtain money, but money is nothing to God. If it is for us and we are putting our trust in Him, He will see to it that we get it. The key is to totally trust Him. Once our faith has been released, then our money will be released. It's not an easy task to walk around blindfold and try to fill your way through life, but releasing faith to God is similar to walking with your eyes closed, your hand stretched out to God, and allowing Him to lead the way. It's hard to trust Him when we walk in an unfamiliar environment. We have to believe He will not let us fall. God, the Great I Am, is everything we need Him to be. We have to believe that He is our Jehovah Jireh, God our Provider. He shall supply all of our need. Not only can He do it, but He will do it.

I cannot recall anyone saying starting a successful business is not complicated. It is truly hard work and it takes much courage. *"Fear not, O land; be glad and rejoice: for the Lord will do great things."* Joel 2:21 is letting us know, despite the destruction of the land, God has not forgotten us and there is about to be a turn around. We are destined for greatness, although our surroundings are showing otherwise. An entrepreneur has to be able to stand against rejection. Everything we want for our business may not come at once, but with perseverance and hard work it will come. We have to look at rejection as a learning experience and press harder. With Jesus on the inside of us, being courageous is in us. We have to learn to reach within ourselves and pull out whatever we need to succeed because it all lies within. In order to get the money we need from an outside source, we first have to have the faith we need in order to believe we can receive that money. There will be times when we are unsure on where to start, who to call, or the necessary steps in going forth to have positive results. *"Call unto me, and I will answer thee, and show thee great and mighty things, which thou knowest not."* Jeremiah 33:3. This scripture instructs us to call on the name of our Lord and He is willing and more than able to show us what we cannot see with our natural eye. Jeremiah 33:3 allows us to know there are great and mighty things out there that we can only know about after calling unto our Lord. Try calling on Jesus and ask Him how to receive money for your business. Have enough faith to believe God will answer you. We cannot put God in a box and narrow down ways on how we think He shall answer. As we call on Him, let's ask the Holy Spirit to give us an ear to hear what the Spirit of the Lord is saying. Therefore, we will know it is Him although the answer may appear to be uncommon.

Wake up was inside of you and present it to the world. The one thing you are so passionate about can be the one thing that causes you to become a millionaire. There are people waiting on you to move, press forward, and bring your dream to life.

Chapter 2

The Vision for Your Business

The vision statement of a business is sometimes called a picture of your company in the future; it is your inspiration, the framework for all your strategic planning. God may give us a vision and we immediately began to think of how awesome it will be to have that vision to be manifested. However, the vision appears to be bigger than you. As you began to meditate on the vision, it becomes clearer and that is when intimidation begins to creep in. Bill Gates envisioned a computer in every place of business and in every home, after he started Microsoft. However, he did not have a series of steps for making that happen. Bill Gates knew what his vision was and how the outcome was supposed to look but not necessarily how he would make it happen. Allowing the Holy Spirit to lead us and guide us, teaches us those things that seemed impossible have now been made possible.

"And the Lord answered me, and said, Write the vision, and make it plain upon tables, that he may run that readeth it. For the vision is yet for an appointed time, but at the end it shall speak, and not lie: though it tarry, wait for it; because it will surely come, it will not tarry." Habakkuk 2:2-3

The purpose for writing your vision is to keep it before you at all times. Confess and thank God for the manifestation of the vision daily. The more we confess what is on paper, the more we will see the manifestation of it. Regardless, of how complicated this process may seem, continue to speak life concerning this vision. As we encounter rejection, speak life. As we encounter doubt, speak life. *"There shall not any man be able to stand before thee all the days of thy life: as I was with Moses so I will be with thee; I will not fail thee, nor forsake thee."* (Joshua 1:5) This word God spoke to Joshua also applies to us. Let us not allow man to put asunder what God has put together. Anyone or anything that tries to come against what God has for us, we need to remember the scripture, "Greater is He that is in me, than he that is in the world." We cast those things back from whence it come and look to God, the author and finisher of our faith.

The way to prosperity is in the Word of God. I am a true witness that God will bring to past our desires when we step out on faith and give Him something to work with. Write the vision and make it plain. Thank God for the vision daily. Walking by faith and not by sight is not looking at stumbling blocks but looking to God. Out of everything God is, failure is not part of Him. God is a God that cannot lie and cannot fail. Why are we such doubters? I constantly tell myself: "God has me, be anxious for nothing, cast my cares on Him." If something does not go right according to my plan, I have to retract and make sure my plan lines up with God's plan. Many times I want things to happen a certain way and I find out God sees otherwise. The end result is always much better than I intended in the beginning. Trusting in God is always the right decision. Once we have our vision, we then give it back to the one who gave it to us. We confess with our mouth and believe in our heart, we will see the manifestation of this business. Pursue every step necessary to bring it into fruition. Do not focus on the complications. Therefore, the complications and setbacks will not become a part of our conversations while discussing our plans with our family and friends. The only time attention is giving to our stumbling blocks is when we are inquiring on how to press pass them.

I was sitting in the "Oasis Christian Center," my local Church home, and I heard Pastor Don Kraft, my Spiritual father, say something that was very profound. The Word He preached gave me new insight on the Word of God. This is what he said: *There are a myriad of places in the Bible where it says the Word is a seed. In 1 Peter1:23, it says the Word is the seed. In Ephesians 5:26, it says The Word of God is water. In Psalms 119:105, it says the Word of God is light. In this Word He has wrapped up everything we need to make it harvest.* So now you may ask yourself about the soil to place the seed in, well that's where we come in. Were we not made from dust or the soil from the ground? We were created to receive the seed, which is the Word of God and because it's an incorruptible seed, it can never die but will only produce. This revelation has motivated me to plant more seed in me, so I can continue to bring forth a harvest in everything I touch. I now study and research the Word in a more discipline way so I can know more about what and Who lives on the inside of me.

Chapter 3

Spending Time with the CEO

"But without faith it is impossible to please Him. For he that cometh to God must believe that He is, and that He is a rewarder of those who diligently seek Him." Hebrews 11:6

There are three different categories a business may fall under, the LLC, Incorporation, and Sole proprietorship. When starting a business one has to decide which category will be a good fit for their business. For whichever category is decided, we have to remember the only way to keep this business abreast is to stay in contact with the creator of the business. God entrusted this in us. He knows we are the one to bring it into fruition. His desire for us is not for us to lose contact with Him. Acknowledging God in all our ways means to rely on Him in total sum. We received the Holy Spirit to teach us, guide us, coach us, and help us to do the will of God.

In corporate America the General Manager hosts meetings with the staff members to talk about goals, success, and status of the company. It is fairly impossible to have a company led by God, but not to spend time with God. This business did not start with just you; therefore, this business cannot carry and be prosperous with just you. God desires our worship. In our worship we invite Him in and we have the ability to receive everything that He is. A healer, deliverer, joyful, and over comer are just a few attributes of Who God is. As we worship God in Spirit and in truth, God reveals Himself to us just as much as we are revealed to Him. Our Lord loves for us to commune with Him. He patiently waits on us to stop all of our fast-paced lives and give Him just a little of that time.

I have always thought there have to be more to life than what I was encountering. As a small child, I would always look for the secret to having a great life. I wanted more for my family and me and often wondered why we were unable to have the greatness (materialistic things) I saw in others. Now that I am older, I have finally found what I have always looked for. It may not be in the form of a chest box filled with gold and precious jewels but it is far greater and it is eternal. The word of God is filled with parables in which leads us into healing, deliverance, prosperity, and eternal glory. The way to come into the knowledge of this is to take the time to worship, pray, and research the meanings of His Holy word. There are many realms of God. Just as we get to the point to where we think we got it, or we think this is it, He takes us a little higher and shows us a little more. The ways of God are everlasting. I am elated to know my Father have endless power.

Everyone is busy. Everyone have so many things to do that it seems there is not enough hours in the day to accomplish all of our tasks. In reality, if we are not taking time from our busy life to spend time with God, then more than likely we are busy doing all the wrong things. How does it profit me to be filled with God and not know what that entails? There are many Christians walking around with the same personality and character as unbelievers. However, maybe some of our brothers and sisters have not taking the time to really get to know what lies within. We have the power to be irate with someone and still walk away. We have the power to forgive and love those that betray us. We have the power to be prosperous during a recession.

It is imperative to allow your CEO to direct each and every strategic move with your business. He knows best. Although it may not make sense or seem logical at the time, our God knows what is ahead of us when we cannot see. During the one on one time with God, surrender your whole heart to Him. Go pass the feelings of what you might sound like or look like and empty yourself on His feet. He desires that from us. During your time of worship, you may not know how to sing, you may not know how to dance, but do you know how to speak? Lie on your face and cry out to your Lord, whatever comes to your heart to say. Tell Him how awesome, great, magnificent, worthy, omnipotent, miraculous, glorious, He is. With the help of the Holy Spirit you have just fawned God. Our God loves the one on one time we give Him. The more time we spend with our CEO, the clearer the vision becomes.

"Now it came to past on the third day, that Esther put on her royal apparel, and stood in the inner court of the king's house: and the king sat upon his royal throne in the royal house, over against the gate of the the house. And it was so, when the king saw Esther the queen standing in the court, that she obtained favor in his sight: and the king held out to Esther the golden sceptre that was in his hand. So Esther drew near, and touched the top of the sceptre. Then said the king unto her, What wilt thou, queen Esther? and what is thy request? it shall be even given thee to the half of the kingdom." *Esther 5:1-3* It is essential for us to put on our garments of worship and enter into our King's house, so that we may obtain favor in His sight. He is waiting on our request. Our praise and worship should now be at a level to where He is saying to us, "whatever you want it is yours, every desire shall be manifested in your life." He seeketh such a worshipper.

Planning one on one time with our Master seems surreal, when we think of the many things we have to get done within twenty-four hours. The best sacrifice we can make is when we choose to put some of those "important" things aside and get with our CEO. One thing about The Holy Spirit being our CEO, unlike other CEOs He will never force meeting times. We have absolute control over the meeting times. However, our businesses may not prosper if we do not receive instruction on how to operate the businesses the true way. According to II Tim. 3:16-17, we may be completely equipped for every good work, because we study the scriptures. We shall be readily prepared to be prosperous and have a life filled with abundance after allowing ourselves to count it worthy to spend time with our Creator.

As we spend time with our CEO, we cannot leave His presence and misrepresent Him. *In all things showing thyself a pattern of good works: in doctrine showing uncorruptness, gravity, sincerity, sound speech, that cannot be condemned; that he that is of the contrary part may be ashamed, having no evil thing to say* (Titus 2:7-8). We cannot control what others might say or think concerning us. However, we can control how we operate or manage our businesses. We have to always make honest decisions and treat others the way we want to be treated when managing a business. The God on the inside of us is a Holy God; likewise, we have to live a holy lifestyle. It is imperative for us to exemplify the characteristics of Jesus Christ.

Having a close relationship with our CEO is essential in having a prosperous business. In some cases it is not about what we know but who we know. Not only knowing but to be in a relationship with the Creator of all is an advantage for us. There are many benefits to having a close relationship with our CEO. Not only will we learn how to have a prosperous business, but we will also learn how to live a Spirit-filled undefeated life. As I consecrate myself and renew my mind I am able to have a positive outlook on the trials and stumbling blocks that appear in my life.

Chapter 4

Hearing Him

"But the Comforter, which is the Holy Ghost, whom the Father will send in my name, he shall teach you all things, and bring all things to your remembrance, whatsoever I have said unto you." John 14:26

The Holy Spirit is sent to lead us and guide us into all truth. Just as the disciples communed with Jesus, we can commune with the Holy Spirit. My prayer is, "Holy Spirit give me an ear to hear what thus saith the Lord." Although we cannot see the Holy Spirit with our natural eye, we have faith to believe He is with us. We have to get into our secret place and allow God to speak to our heart and mind in order to endure life as it unfolds. There are times when we feel as though we do not know if God is speaking. I hear people say they are not absolute sure if it was God or just a passing thought. When you have a thought that lines up with the word of God and it is a faith move, it is more likely to be the Holy Spirit speaking to your heart. Before coming into the knowledge of how God will speak to me, I would have a passing thought concerning a decision, a person, or my life. I would then say to myself this cannot be or why am I thinking like this. I would soon ignore the thought and brush it away. Only to find out later, the still small voice

I heard was the Spirit of God and I should have taken heed to what I heard Him speak to my heart.

Learning to walk by faith teaches us every thought and action is based on how we believe. It all sums up to truly trusting God and knowing He is God. One day as I was pulling up to my workplace, I did not see any vacant parking spots available where I wanted to park. I wanted to park close to the building because I knew when my shift was over it would be dark. The next available parking lot required me to have to walk behind another building. I did not want to park that far away. After I pulled up to the parking lot where I wanted to park and noticed no available parking spaces, I also noticed there was not anyone in sight. My first thought was no one will be leaving anytime soon. I sat in my car gathering all my things together. I heard in my heart, "when you are finished gathering all your things and completely ready to get out the car, there will be a parking space available." I turned my car off and sat there finishing up some things I needed to do before I got out the car. Within two minutes, I was completely finished. I looked up and a girl came around the building getting in her car to leave. I started to praise God and I said, "wow, God that was really You I heard in my heart." I then heard the Spirit of the Lord say; "I'm teaching you to trust me wholeheartedly in everything." I am truly in awe of God. Based on human reasoning, I would have pulled off from the building the moment I got there because I could not see anyone. God sees what we cannot see. He is an on time God. He may not come when we want Him to come, but He comes when He needs to come. I didn't really need the parking space until I was ready to get out the car. My thought was I needed it before I really needed it. God always knows what is best for our lives.

"For My thoughts are not your thoughts, nor are your ways My ways," says the Lord. For as the heavens are higher than the earth, so are My ways higher than your ways, and my thoughts than your thoughts." Isaiah 55:8-9. Our God's thoughts are unimaginable to our thoughts. There is a limit to how far out thoughts can reach. We serve a limitless God, which means there is no limit on anything concerning Him. In order to retrieve the immeasurable thoughts the Spirit of the Lord wants to share with us, we need to have a relationship with Him. A renewed mind allows us to keep our "spiritual eyes" open. The enemy will try and use anything he thinks will work to try and distract us. Hearing and being led by the Holy Spirit will elude us from any tactic the enemy tries to use. In that moment, it may appear the enemy is winning or may have gotten the best of you, however, just as Joseph told his brothers that wanted to kill him in Genesis 50:20, "you thought evil against me; but God meant it unto good." Our great God can turn any situation around and receive glory from it. He is an omnipotent God.

Trusting and hearing God with our whole life is metaphorically like putting on a blindfold in the morning and allowing someone to lead you everywhere you are suppose to go throughout the day. We have to believe God has us and will direct us accordingly. Apostle Don Kraft, my spiritual father, always talk about how we are our own prophet. We have to prophesy to ourselves. What we speak over our life, good or bad, will be manifested. We have to confess God's word daily. Meditate on His word day and night. Declare and decree to the atmosphere who God says you are. By faith, move on that word, stand on that word, and continue to believe on that word. Have enough confidence in yourself to believe you can hear God. Anything that does not line up with the word of God and does not bring forth life, cast it down. God's words always bring forth life. As a Christian, there are many benefits we are entitled to have. I choose to take advantage of every benefit and live an abundant life. My family and I go on vacation once a year. I like to stay in resorts with many amenities, places in which, breakfast, indoor pool, and workout rooms are included. If the rate at my resort has all those things included, why would I leave my resort to go down the street to buy breakfast, pay to swim or workout elsewhere? I had already paid the price when I booked my stay. It would be foolish of me to purchase those things and not use them. Jesus paid the price so we cannot only have life but to also have it more abundantly. I choose to take Him up on that. Today is a good day for us to seek how to have that abundant life. Having a true relationship with our Heavenly Father and searching His word daily is a great way to start.

In my life, I find it imperative to have a very good Bible teaching church home. There are times when I read scriptures and I just cannot seem to get a clear understanding of what I'm reading. After attending my church home, the following Wednesday or Sunday, my Pastor will begin to read, teach, and expound on what I read during the week. That is enough confirmation for me to know God knows, hears, and cares about everything concerning me. I cannot reiterate enough on how important it is for us to step out on faith, trust God, and do our part. It does not matter how big or small it appears we have to make the effort and show God we are truly willing.

Human reasoning can cause our businesses to remain a mere thought. A renewed mind and putting feet to our faith is what causes our mere thought to become realistic prosperous businesses. We have to learn to "think outside the box." Our God can speak to our hearts and give us a life changing command that typically does not make sense to the average man. It is not for us to analyze and bring forth a logical meaning to what we believe God have spoken to us. It is meant for us to pray and make sure it is God, then move on His command. He always has provision, although we may not always see it in the beginning. Therefore, move on His command and watch the puzzle pieces come together.

Chapter 5

Facing Rejection

"And I will make thee exceeding fruitful, and I will make nations of thee, and kings shall come out of thee." Genesis 17:6

We are destined to be great. God created us in His image. In the depths of us are kings that are waiting to come forth. How can a man bring forth a king except he be a king? The days are here where we see ourselves the way God sees us. The time when we look in the mirror and only see our physical appearance is outdated. Let's look past the flesh and see who we really are. We need to now come into the knowledge of knowing we are spiritual beings with a temporary body, not bodies with a temporary spirit. The more we look to God the more we see God. Our renewed minds have brought forth newness in our hearts. Look in God, see your reflection, and write down what you see. Call forth what you see and continue the confessions until it has been manifested. We do not have to wait on God, God is waiting on us. *"Therefore say unto them, Thus saith the Lord God; There shall none of my words be prolonged any more, but the word which I have spoken shall be done, saith the Lord God."* Ezekiel 12:28

Search within, the thing that intimidates you the most; the part of you that is being suppressed because of intimidation, fear of others opinions, etc. could be the very thing that will bring a level of success to your life. Saying things to yourself such as, "I can never do that, who am I to make that happen, surely someone else would have come up with this if it is so brilliant." Or maybe even thinking, "What if I fail, what if this does not work?" Thoughts such as these creeping inside of us is a CLEAR indication that it will work, it is God, and you have what it takes to make your business become a success.

Once we have cast down dark thoughts, the next step is research. Whatever it is God has put on your heart to bring forth, start inquiring everything it is to know about it. Research trademarks and patents to see if it is something already out there. If not, then you get it patented. *"and whatsoever ye do, do it heartily, as to the Lord, and not unto men; knowing that of the Lord ye shall receive the reward of the inheritance: for ye serve the Lord Christ." Colossians 3: 23-24.* Allow God to see you are making an effort and walking by faith, although you do not know exactly what to do. The Holy Spirit will then start dropping things in your Spirit and strategically moving on your behalf. More ideas will then begin to come and it will no longer appear as a farfetched fiction thought. There are times we have such great ideas and business ventures, but we wait for them to just happen without putting forth an effort. I have learned waiting on things to just happen never works for me. We have to believe in God first, and believe in ourselves second. If Bill Gates can be successful, we can be prosperous. If Oprah Winfrey, Steve Harvey, or the business owner down the street can have success, we can have it also. God have no respect of persons. God freely gives. Since we only have this one life to live, why not go ahead and make it great?

Rejection does not feel good; however, it shows us we are stronger than we thought. The moment we realize rejection will not kill us, we need to press pass our emotions and try harder the next moment. Let's think back of all the times we were rejected. It appears to be more than we can count on both hands, but praise our Holy Jesus; we are still here and moving forward. This means rejection could not stop us. I often go out and pursue business opportunities in my community. I present my business to other companies to get sales. I usually feel really good about my presentations. There are times when these other companies are not interested in what I have to say. Encountering negative responses from some of these companies sometimes makes me feel like a failure. During those times, I usually go to my car, give myself a small pity party, and then I pray. My prayer helps me to realize I serve a God who cannot fail. I serve an all-knowing God, One in which only wants the best for me. I have those moments when I get down and feel bad about myself. Those moments pass. It is imperative not to speak out on those feelings usually attached with rejection. The words that come from our lips hold so much power. We have to be aware of what and how we speak things. *"For he that will love life, and see good days, let him refrain his tongue from evil, and his lips that they speak no guile."* 1 Peter 3:10; we have to focus on not allowing negativity, rejection, and doubt to come from our lips. A renewed mind is the technique used to help keep us focused.

Intimidation can grow into a huge giant, if we allow it to creep in. We have to denounce it before it appears. The steps that usually shut down a business before it starts are listed below:

Step 1: Doubt-*A feeling of uncertainty or lack of conviction*

An example of having doubt is: Who am I to make this happen? If this idea was so great, someone else would have thought of it.

Step 2: Disbelief- *Inability or refusal to accept that something is true or real.*

An example to having disbelief is, I can never make that happen, besides where will I ever get the funds for this?

Step 3: Intimidation- *To make timid or fearful.*

An example of feeling intimidated by your business idea will cause you to have thoughts such as; *this idea appears to be bigger than I can ever be.* The more we think on how to start this business, the bigger it seems to get. We then become smaller in our eyes, facing something so big we run from it. This have just caused us to be inferior mentally, we pushed this idea back deep into our soul, that now it becomes a passing thought every so often.

Today we break this cycle off of our life. Today we make a conscious decision to walk in the perfect will of God. Let's start by making this confession: "Nothing and no one will frustrate the plan of God for my life, not even me." This confession is basically saying, what God has for me will be manifested in my life regardless of what today looks like. The more we confess this, the more we will believe this and it will become our reality. In Genesis 1:3, God said, "let there be light, and it was so." He spoke it and it was so. Because we were created in His image, we can speak a business and it will be so.

We are our own prophet. There are people who travel miles to allow a prophet to speak in their life. I anticipate the day we have enough confidence in the God in us to speak in our own life. Command your heart and soul to line up with God's perfect will for your life. Cast down any negative words that try to rise within you. Without an open heart and a renewed mind, we are limited of what we can become. The sky is not the limit for the confidence and faith we have in ourselves. God can help us with our unbelief if we ask Him. We can go into a place in God to where certain things just cannot touch us. Once the devil sees that nothing can strike our confidence level, and he cannot move us, he has to move to the next person. God is waiting on us. He has promised to never leave nor forsake us. When you feel there is a distant between you and God, know that you have wandered off.

People and things can distract us from what God have commanded us to do. Distraction comes in a variety of faces. Staying focus for many is work; some of us have to make a conscious decision to stay focused. It is not easy to have a tunnel mind on this journey. I remember times I have knowingly allowed distraction to come in because I was fearful of doing what I knew God was requiring of me. I did not want to face rejection and I did not have enough faith to believe God had my back. I was very excited the day I learned I could cast my cares on Jesus and did not have to carry that stress anymore. I praise Jesus for deliverance. I now know I can be a trendsetter. I can be the first to make things happen and I no longer have to follow the lead of someone else all the time. There are times when I am supposed to lead and its okay. I am in a place in my life where I can boldly stand up and stand out without fear of rejection. I no longer care who likes me or who disagrees with me. I stand on the word of God and know in Whom I know. If my experiment does not work the way I think it should, I can say I know because I tried, not because of doubt. People will always be people and God will always be God. When we turn to people they may or may not come through for us, but when we turn to God, He is always there. In some cases, peoples' intentions are good, but life happens to everyone and sometimes unknown, unpredictable, spontaneous things happen to others when you needed them to be there for you. We cannot get mad at people for being people. We have to realize sometimes when we are depending on people; God wants us to depend on him. When we turn to God, we know He is the same yesterday, today, and forever more. He may not always come at the moment we want Him to come. However, we find out He is always right on time. Just as Elijah commanded the rain to stop until he saw otherwise, I can command prosperous doors to open for me. He has no respect of persons. It is all about my belief system. I believe God for what I always thought was impossible. I confess my dreams into reality. I prophesy my faith to rise up in me to believe I cannot only have one prosperous business but many prosperous businesses.

Chapter 6

Believe God

Through faith we understand the world was framed by the word of God, so things which are seen were not made of things which do appear." The message Bible translates this scripture as, "By faith, we see the world called into existence by God's word, what we see created by what we don't see." We have the power to see concrete manifestations of our confessions based on our abstract faith. We have to believe in the God inside of us enough to believe in ourselves. It is easy to believe and have faith in others because of their history. Based on the history of our jobs, we know at a certain time on a certain day we will receive a paycheck. We also know by the history of our postman, he will bring our mail at a certain time. By the history of our God, we should have faith to believe He wants us to prosper and it can happen for us.

Many of us say we are waiting on promises from God. In reality, we are waiting on ourselves to have enough faith to believe the promises can be manifested. *"And Jesus said unto them, because of your unbelief: for verily I say unto you, If ye have faith as a grain of mustard seed, ye shall say unto this mountain, remove hence to yonder place; and it shall remove; and nothing shall be impossible onto you."* Mathew 17:20. God will speak a word to our heart and we have to believe it will be manifested. I have experienced when the Holy Spirit gave me a word for an individual and I did not obey, someone else came and gave the same word to the individual. God wants a willing vessel to bring forth His vision. If it is meant to be, it will be, with or without us.

Witty inventions and great business ideas coming to you can mean God has entrusted you to make it happen. The provision is there. The train business we have has become a huge success in our community. We are the first to have a train business in our city. One of our trains is located at a local outside mall. I was driving the train one day and a woman began to motion for me. As I approached her, I saw a puzzled look on her face. She started to tell me she has never seen the train out there and wanted to know how long had it been there. I had only been there for a few months at the time. The woman had a regretful appearance and began shaking her head. I asked her was everything okay and she told me she had the same idea as I about the train business one year prior. She said she wanted to put a train in the exact mall, but she was too busy to research information regarding the trains. She also said, she asked her husband to start looking into it and he just never did it. If she had moved on her idea, there is a possibility my train would not have been out there, or it was never meant for her to be there because it was ordained for me.

Everything we need to live a prosperous, successful, conquering life is placed on the inside of us, once we have accepted Jesus Christ as our personal Lord and Savior. After receiving Jesus, we need to capture a renewed mind by seeking whole truth from the word of God. That is the key to walking victoriously on this Earth. We have to truly walk by faith and not by sight. I cannot tell God I believe His word, yet my actions show otherwise. I must go forward in what I believe until I see the manifestation of it. As I go forward, sometimes it appears the blind spots are overwhelming. During those times, I stop and allow God to take my hand and lead me out of the darkness. Having a train business in my community appears to be unique. When I present my business to some they began to question how this did come about. Some responses are, "wow, this is different and creative." One lady told me she never would have thought God was in the train business, which seems too simple for God. God knows how to make things that seem so deep to be so simple.

Chapter 7

Go Forth

"What is man, that thou art mindful of him? And the son of man, that thou visitest him? For thou hast made him a little lower than the angels, and hast crowned him with glory and honor. Thou madest him to have dominion over the works of thy hands; thou has put all things under his feet." Psalms 8:4-6

No w that I know I have dominion over all the works of my hands, I can stop living a seemingly defeated life. My God have entrusted me to be ruler over all His works on this Earth. It is time for me to start ruling and making better judgment decisions. Knowledge is power. Reading the word of God, gives us knowledge and understanding on how we are to go about daily and be prosperous in everything we do. Looking over my life, it appears I have had no authority. However, by faith, I have all authority to possess whatever I want as long as it lines up with the word of God. We can hold our God accountable for His word. We can remind God how we are the seed of Abraham, Possessor of Heaven and Earth. The Bible says God have no respect of persons. We have to believe and stand on what is written. If I can believe God for one Scripture, I can believe Him for all Scriptures. Psalms 37:4 says to *"Delight thyself also in the Lord; and he shall give thee the desires of thine heart."* When we are delighted in God, He has placed those desires in our hearts. Therefore, we are able to bring them into existence.

We have the power and God have given the provision. In order to see the provision, we first have to make our faith move. We have the feet of warriors. We possess the land our feet tread upon. Today is the day to stop allowing others to take our land. Let's believe we receive the word of God and hold on to it. We have to give God something to work with. We have to search the scriptures and apply them to our life. We can remind God of His word and what He promises us so we can see the manifestation of it. We have waited and dreamed for years. Now we can put feet to our visions and command them to walk. *"And God said, Let there be light: and there was light."* We as Christians believe the same God that created the Heaven and Earth is the same God we are made in the image of. He commanded and it was so. We too can command and it be so. The key to such a prosperous life is to have the faith to believe we can receive. *"Therefore let no man glory in men: for all things are yours; whether Paul, or Apollos, or Cephas, or the world, or life, or death, or things present, or things to come; all are yours; and ye are Christ's; and Christ's is God's."* I cor. 3:21-23 says because we are in Christ, everything belongs to us. Are we not the seed of Abraham? Having Christ in us is huge. 1 Cor. 3:21-23 have just told us that all things belong to us. What are we going to do with this revelation? Let us go forth and receive what have been already given to us. No more defeated life! No more negative thinking! It is our decision to accept or not accept what has been given to us. Our world is framed from our level of faith (Heb. 11:3). Some of us walk in a small frame because we have small faith. It is never too late to increase our level of faith.

We are destined to be entrepreneurs. Why should others have what belongs to us. Stop working for someone else eight hours a day and have others work for you, if that's your desire. The world is waiting for you to bring forth those million dollar ideas you possess. It is great to be content in whatever situation we are in, yet we always have to strive for more. Our destiny is calling for us to move right now. *"And so he that had received five talents came and brought other five talents saying, Lord, thou deliveredst unto me five talents: behold, I have gained beside them five talents more. His Lord said unto him, well done, thou good and faithful servant: thou hast been faithful over a few things, I will make thee ruler over many things: enter thou into the joy of the Lord."* What will we do with what God has given us? When will we proceed and increase our talents that God has bestowed in us? How will God respond to us?

Afterword

Starting a Business Allowing the Holy Spirit to be Your CEO was written to encourage others as well as myself, if we have received Jesus for our Lord and Savior, all things are possible. Having a relationship with the Holy Spirit and being sensitive to hear what thus saith the Lord, allows us to live an abundant life. Starting and having a successful business is not easy, however, being led by the Holy Spirit will prepare us for all the mishaps, stumbling blocks, and rejections that are there and can so easily distract us. My husband and I were working full-time jobs barely having money to pay our bills. I had never desired my own business in the past. I never thought it to be possible for me. As I prayed to God, one day on my way to work, I explained to Him I was tired of struggling, not having enough money, and I desired more. From that moment up until now, my life has never been the same. I want this book to help you become the person you were destined to be and I also want you to see yourself having the business you dream about daily. This book is about starting a business allowing the Holy Spirit to lead and guide your constant steps. More importantly, this book helps and teaches on how to become closer to Christ. We should all be enjoying the abundant life (the life in God that makes God, God) Jesus came for us to have.

My Moment

I use to stare out of my dad's apartment window, when I was a little girl. He lived on the second floor in an apartment complex in my hometown. I will never forget how I use to look out the living room window and stare at the distant highway. I would always speculate the whereabouts of the passing traffic. I would ask myself, "What is going on that I'm missing out on." I would then have thoughts on where I could be or what I would be doing if I were somewhere else. When I became a young adult, and had my own apartment, I would stand in my bedroom, which was on the second floor, and stare at the distant traffic as I did when I was a child. Again, I would wonder where all the vehicles were headed and what I'm possibly missing out on. I would also think about the things I could or would be doing if I was somewhere else. Now at the age of thirty-six, for the first time in my life, I stare out the window of the second floor of my two-story home. As I watch the passing traffic on the distant highway, I have no desire to care where the vehicles are going. I watch the vehicles and feel as though whatever is going on outside of where I am, I am at peace knowing that I am exactly where I am suppose to be. It is amazing to come to a place in life where you know and feel you are right where God will have you.

My Moment

I sit and reflect back on my life and began to read my journal. I began to read what I wrote in my journal on April 18, 2007. *Lord God, I thank you for this season in my life. God I know I have relocated for such a time as this. I have been separated from all of my familiarity. I thank you for all the alone time I am able to spend with You. I know the way to get to know a person is to spend time with that person. I thank You God that I am truly getting to know You. It doesn't matter what it looks like, I believe this is my place of prosperity.*

I wrote this during a time when I made a huge transition and by faith I had to believe God everything would come together. Despite, the circumstances that were coming against me, I believed and walked by faith, things were going to become better for me. Today, the better has been manifested.

Printed in the United States
By Bookmasters